I0177494

CHRISTIANITY

NOT

CHRISTENDOM.

By J. N. DARBY.

LONDON:

G. MORRISH, 24, WARWICK LANE,

PATERNOSTER ROW.

CHRISTIANITY NOT CHRISTENDOM.

THE times in which we are, the question in every serious
·man's mind is, " Are we to go back to popery or not?"
the fears of surprised protestants; and the insolent pre-
tensions of papists and puseyites; while the only thing
that has courage by their side is infidelity, and indiffer-
ence to truth, which rather favours error than truth
because truth is truth, and insists on itself; the heart-
sickening imbecility of those who govern, or rather,
who are afraid to govern; the solemn sight that courage
is found only on the side of evil, so that it looks like the
judgment of God—leads one to ask, What is this church
so vaunted by dishonest puseyites, and honest Roman
Catholics, or those who from its prestige and influence,
whatever that prestige and influence may be, cling to it,
while they do not believe one word about it, for such is
the case very widely in Roman Catholic countries—what
is this church, this great system, which carries such
weight with men?

We must not suppose that anglicans, or evangelicals,
or dissenters, have escaped its influence; they may be
anxious to avoid its being quite popish, or to lower its
condition to open infidelity. Men may be high church
or broad church, Roman or Greek, but they are all
church of some kind, or would be. They may have
altars instead of tables, or cry establishments down, but
if they do, they will dignify the once modest chapel

with the name of church. What is this church? that word that has such charm in it; is it something from God, and of God as it stands?

That it has some charm in it is evident from the well-known fact that whereas in the popular English Bible of the day, there was "congregation" where now we have "church;" king James insisted that church and only church should be there. It has a successional character, and however small the rivulet in which some think to have pure water, still it is to be derived from larger ones into channels that, they pretend, makes the water pure. The grosser corruptions were purged away three centuries ago; what resulted has largely turned to infidelity, and many are going back to the superstitions as that which is in the old channel.

What is this great system, this potent idea? Is a successional church, corrupt or purified or infidelized (if I may coin a new word for a new state of things), a church of the past, on a pattern some centuries ago, or a church of the future, with no pattern at all but man's fancied competency in this age to do better and be wiser than all before him; is any church as now understood, coming down from ages past, however reformed and arranged, a thing of God? Is it to pass in some shape on this descendible principle? Is there that which, calling itself a church, exercises authority over the mind of man according to the mind of God? We are forced to look the whole question in the face: is the existing professing church, whatever shape it may assume, a thing which God owns? Is a successional body in any shape true or right according to God? I repeat, this question is forced upon us, the whole question; not Is this or that church right?

The universal confession, Greek rejecting Rome, puseyites coyly flirting with it, protestants abhorring it, dissenters seeking to pull down what exists, because it stands in their way, joining Rome for this purpose, episcopalians trying to keep it together, truth or no truth, Rome itself divided through idolatry of the Virgin, and infallibility of the pope, which notoriously contradicts all history, yet increasing her sway in the world, all in confusion as all admit from the pope to dissenters, all wanting to have the church right, though all for very different reasons thinking its state wrong ; making the inquiry as to which is right hopeless. They have raised the question : what is it they are fighting about ? Each party, no doubt, trust themselves ; but every man's hand is against his neighbour, and how is the sober looker-on to trust them ?

I am well aware that the good churchman will tell me that this is the effect of schism, and that people have what calls itself the church to look to ; but how am I to know which is the church ? I am told there are marks of it, yet who is to assign the true ones ? But be it so, catholicity is one of them, that is universality : but more than half professing Christendom is outside what pretends to be it, and hundreds of thousands of its most respectable members leaving it as corrupt. Sanctity ? But history shews it to have been the most unholy thing that ever existed. Apostolic succession ? A man must be a learned man to know if it exist, and if he is, he will know it did not ; that nothing is more uncertain, if not certain that it is broken ; besides, to make my salvation depend on the right succession of a set of wicked men, who put down one another in the dark ages, is rather too strong. Then, unity ? The oldest churches, the Greek, counting by millions, reject and denounce it. Unity, holiness, catholicity, are a fable as regards the church; excellent, blessed things, only not to be found now-a-days.

The conscience of half Europe rose against the open, flagrant, impious iniquity of what they call the church; nay, take it altogether, the change of system shews, at the rate it has gone on, that the boasted church could not take care of its children, was incompetent to prevent the mischief. All we simple people know is, that *Quicquid delirant reges plectuntur Achivi.* The church cannot be trusted, it has not been able somehow to take care of itself. In Roman Catholic countries, and now also in protestant ones, not only scientific men, but masses of the uneducated are turned, or turning infidels, and the remedy is, superstitious ceremonies and a going back to what was so notoriously corrupt that natural conscience would stand it no longer; when to be a clergyman, or of religion, was universally to be esteemed worthless, submitted to for the necessities of sacramental grace, and despised for licensed and unlicensed immorality.

And this was the church. Is this what we are reduced to? or to turn infidel and deny the Saviour that loved us and gave Himself for us? Assuredly not. The truth is as true as ever, divine love as full, above all our evil, the Lord as sure in His faithfulness, His arm unshortened. But the church, so called, cannot help us; it cannot help itself. Which church am I to trust to? Who will tell me? *The* church, I am told. Where is it? In Rome? No, cry loudly both the most ancient church, the Greek, and all the protestants, who have more or less purified themselves from it, unless in despair of themselves they are going back to it, and now many of the most respectable of themselves who have broken with it. From Rome to which am I to go? Who will tell me that? I have a din of voices claiming to be right. We want Christianity not Christendom, we have had enough of that.

Now I look all this in the face and take the question up, not on the disputed claims of churches, who mutually disprove their respective claims, but on the question of *the* church, as man looks at it now, as we see it in every time as the subject of ecclesiastical history, and I say it never was, as a system, the institution of God, or what God established; but at all times, from its first appearance in ecclesiastical history, the departure, as a system, from what God established. and nothing else: primitive church and all; and the more it was formally established, the more it was corrupt. Saints, beloved of God, I do not doubt were and are in it, but it was a corruption offensive to God from the beginning of its history; take a history, any history, of the church, it is a history, not of God's institution. but of man's corruption. History and scripture both testify of this, and no man can speak of the church of ecclesiastical history, if he be an honest man, without admitting, that it was man's corruption, not God's institution, or denying history and scripture alike; I say, from its outset as the subject of ecclesiastical records, or scripture statements.

That Christ has a church which He loved and gave Himself for, and will present to Himself a glorious church, no true Christian denies; nor that the work which gathered it was to be carried on on earth, nor that in a scriptural sense the foundation was laid on earth : all that is true: but my proposition is simple, the church as the subject of history never was anything but man's corruption; the people who composed it went on, but the moment it was left to man's responsibility it departed from God's principles.

Let not my reader be surprised. Let us speak of man. What is man before our eyes and the subject of history and of God's dealings? Is he, was he ever, in his actual history, God's creature as He set him up? Never! He is the corruption of what God set up and nothing else, save that one blessed One who came to save. Let me draw attention to a great principle running through scripture, that surprise may be less at my assertion, which may naturally astound many, so much do we cling to tradition; and here even an infidel may recognize, not the truth of God of course, the principle that runs through what the believer owns, what I own, as a divine revelation: that principle is that *in every case* God set up that which was good positively or relatively, and the first thing man did was to corrupt and ruin it; and then history is the history of man's corrupt condition, though, no doubt, so much the more of God's patience and goodness.

Man was set up good: the first thing he did was to fall into sin and corrupt himself; his history is the history of a fallen race; God judged that world. I am putting the scripture account of what has always happened; not discussing its truth, but giving its view of what has taken place. Noah was spared from a ruined world and government set up as restraint to man's passions; the first thing he does after his burnt offering, that is stated in scripture—mind I am giving *its* view of things—is to get drunk, and we hear no more of him, and the world goes on to Babel and confusion.

The law was given when God called out a people for Himself, the world being gone into idolatry, worshipping stocks and stones and given up to a reprobate mind: before Moses comes down from the mount with the two tables of the law, the people have made a golden calf and have cast off God altogether.

The priesthood was set up, consecrated of God: the first day after the consecration was complete, two of them offer strange fire, and Aaron never entered into the holy of holies in his robes of glory and beauty; was excluded from all ordinary access to God.

Royalty was set up; the Son of David was to be God's king, build his temple, and be every way blessed. He loves many strange women, turns to idolatry and the kingdom is ruined. God afterwards transfers power to the Gentiles, sets up the head of gold, leaving Jerusalem, casting down David's throne; and men often think, if despotic, they would do all manner of wise and good things, but Nebuchadnezzar casts the faithful into the fire and gets in every sense a beast's heart; Gentile power is corrupt, ambitious and violent; cannot, as scripture speaks, stay at home, what it describes by likening them to ravening beasts.

Such is the uniform account given me in scripture of what has gone on, God's ways, and man's ways when God has set up anything; I am not saying anything of grace on His part—it exalts it—but of His public dealings and man's conduct when God had instituted anything on earth, of man's history. Is it very surprising if the same thing has happened in Christianity? No doubt vastly increased light and an altogether fuller revelation of grace are found in Christianity. It was the revelation of God, not the government of man as he was, or law suited to him; but this is not the question, but, what man has been when this was committed to him; when he was placed under responsibility in respect of this revelation. Nor could I, nor could any, thank God, deny that there were saints when the general standing was one of total failure, and, in principle, apostasy from the first estate: there was Abel, and Noah, and Enoch, after the fall, and even fuller testimony as evil closed in, and Elijah's when Israel, in one sense because Israel, had made the golden calves and gone after Baal; but that is not the question, but, what was the state of things?

Now I shall first present the historical fact, before I quote the instructions of scripture on the subject; but scripture must itself tell us both the basis from which men fell away and some of the facts too; now Galatians, without going into the higher doctrines of Ephesians and Colossians, will afford us the great foundational basis, and in a measure what departure from it is. Two great principles lie at the base of Christianity, God's righteousness, Christ sitting at the right hand of God, and the presence of the Holy Ghost: Paul tells us (2 Cor. iii.) that Christianity or the gospel was the ministration of righteousness and the ministration of the Spirit; these are the two great essential elements. So again—but now the righteousness of God without the law is manifested; and again to declare, I say, at this time His righteousness; and, the righteousness of God by faith of Jesus Christ. So Philippians iii.—not having mine own righteousness which is by the law, but that which is through the faith of Christ, the righteousness which is of God by faith. Christ has made peace by the blood of His cross and left peace to His disciples. Peace was what was preached and remission of sins: being justified by faith, says the apostle, we have peace with God, Christ having borne our sins on His own body on the tree.

The cross had told what man was; he had there rejected God's Son, His last messenger to seek fruit from men as such; and God's work of redemption and peace-making was wholly finished there, so that believers are reconciled to God, have no more conscience of sins. In Him we have redemption through His blood, even the forgiveness of sins according to the riches of His grace; redeemed by the precious blood of Christ, as of a lamb without blemish and without spot. They that are sanctified are perfected for ever by one offering, and the Holy Ghost is a witness that our sins and iniquities are remembered no more; yea, we have boldness for the day of judgment, because as He (Christ) is, so are we in this world. It is on the work of grace in Christ that the apostle rests, and assures us of the blessedness of the man to whom the Lord imputes no sin, our being justified by faith: Abraham believed God and it was counted to him for righteousness.

Now in the Galatian assemblies the Judaizing teachers had introduced the doctrine of righteousness by the law; and this the apostle earnestly combats. In no epistle do we find the anxiety that is in this, not a salutation at the end, not a kind word at the beginning, but absorbed by the fatal subversion of Christianity that had got in amongst them, he plunges at once into his subject—" I marvel that ye are so soon removed from him that called you into the grace of Christ unto another gospel, which is not another; but there be some that trouble you and would pervert the gospel of Christ: but though we, or an angel from heaven, preach any other gospel unto you than that which we have preached unto you, let him be accursed. As we said before so say I now again, If any man preach any other gospel unto you than that which ye have received let him be accursed."

He then goes on laboriously to deny any succession from the apostles; he had received neither the truth nor office from them: he was not of man nor by man, but by Jesus Christ and God the Father. His adversaries insisted on succession in the ministry and ordination, but he indignantly repudiated it; but the main point which he declared was, the subversion of Christianity was the introduction of righteousness by works of law, or law in any shape: it was frustrating, setting aside, and making void (οὐκ ἀθετῶ) the grace of God, for if righteousness came by law, Christ was dead in vain: that as many as were of the works of the law were under the curse. This was the great thesis of the apostle: Christ is become of no effect unto you; as many of you as are justified by the law, ye are fallen from grace. And what he especially appeals to in testimony of this is, that they had received the Holy Ghost as the seal of this doctrine of being justified by faith and not by works of law; the presence of the Holy Ghost and the way it came decided the question.

I do not question fruits of a new nature would follow demonstrating that the faith is real, and that the Christian has to shew his faith by his works, but never by works of law, the works which God delights in are alone those which are the fruit of faith; the christian is bound, and disposed if he is one, to do good works; you do right to claim them from him, but why? because he is a Christian first. People have forgotten the simple principle that duties flow from the relationships we are already in, and cannot exist for us till we are in those relationships. I say this much to avoid mistakes, but it is not my subject; man had duties as man, but he has failed in them; he is a sinner, and is lost, according to Christianity. The full exposition given in the Romans on this great point is, that Gentiles were lawless, the Jews law-breakers; that there was none righteous, no, not one; that every mouth was stopped and all the world guilty before God; all had sinned and come short of the glory of God; being justified freely by His grace through the redemption that was in Christ Jesus. And Christianity teaches us that the blessed Son of God finished the work which His Father gave Him to do; and we read that by Him all that believe are justified from all things from which they could not be justified by the law of Moses; that when He had by Himself purged our sins He sat down at the right hand of God; that if this whole work of making peace and perfecting the believers for ever were not accomplished by His one offering, He must have suffered often.

We have seen that it is by faith that we are justified, redemption is through His blood, and hence the believer's being justified through faith, reconciled to God, having peace with God, is one great pillar of Christianity, Christianity itself as a foundation including the blessed revelation of the Father in the Son: for it is not as slighting His blessed person that I speak of His work, but when grace has drawn the heart to own His person, the gospel is the answer to the need the revelation of His person has created. So the poor woman in the city that was a sinner drawn in deep humiliation to His person receives the answer, "thy sins are forgiven thee, thy faith hath saved thee, go in peace;" the thief who owned Him Lord and the Man who had done nothing amiss, and looked for the kingdom received the blessed answer "To-day shalt thou be with me in paradise."

The other great truth which constitutes Christianity is, the presence of the Holy Ghost; that the believer receives, so that he is sealed with it and that the Spirit dwells in him. We have a kind of picture of the connection of both in John xx., when the Lord first says to Mary Magdalene to tell His brethren "I go to my Father and your Father, my God and your God;" and, then, when they gather He is there and says to them, "Peace be unto you," and "as my Father hath sent me so send I you. And when he had said this he breathed on them and saith unto them, Receive ye the Holy Ghost." I merely take the general thought that we get the disciples, the brethren, put into the same relationship to God and the Father as Christ Himself, peace proclaimed to them and the Holy Ghost communicated to them.

I return to the Galatians, to which I first referred. We have seen how the apostle makes justification by faith a question of Christianity, or the contrary, and this we have seen confirmed by a crowd of passages, and divine righteousness put as the answer to there being none righteous, no, not one, amongst men, and this by the work of Christ effectual to us by faith, so that we are perfected for ever by one offering, and no sin imputed to us. The apostle shews how this is no allowance of sin, but the way of power against it, in Romans vi., only here I confine myself to the point in hand.

Now let us see what is said as to the Holy Spirit. This is directly everywhere connected with the exaltation of Christ as man to the right hand of God; that when man in the person of the Lord Jesus was exalted to the right hand of God, in virtue of His perfectly glorifying God on the cross, the Holy Ghost was sent down here to dwell in them that believe, and that this made the distinctive difference of Christians and Christianity: divine righteousness having placed man on high as the result of a work done for man's salvation and blessing, the Holy Ghost was given to those that believed. Let us proceed to cite the proofs; they may be multiplied, but the principal ones are so clear and definite that I need not go through them, though the distinctive character of the presence of the Holy Ghost marking out the essential difference of Christianity will be clearer the more we are acquainted with the Old and New Testaments. The promise of the Holy Ghost in the Old Testament, as characterizing Christianity, is sufficiently demonstrated by Peter's quotation of Joel: "It shall come to pass in the last days I will pour out of my Spirit upon all flesh; and your sons and your daughters shall prophesy, and your young men shall see visions, and your old men shall dream dreams, and on my servants and on my handmaids will I pour out in those days of my Spirit." It is only needful to remark that it was upon *all*, young and old, servants and handmaids, no trace of a clergy or body to whom it was limited, but formally the contrary: nor was it then only the apostles, there were a hundred and twenty there, and women among them. The Lord Himself had promised it: "If any man thirst let him come unto me and drink, and, as the scripture hath said, out of his belly shall flow rivers of living water; this spake he of the Spirit which they that believe on him should receive, for the Holy Ghost was not yet [given, οὔπω ἦν], because Jesus was not yet glorified;" what was known as the Holy Ghost thus present among them was not yet.

And this is what the twelve disciples at Ephesus say : not, we have not so much as heard whether there be any Holy Ghost, but whether the Holy Ghost is (come); they were John's disciples, and he had spoken of baptizing with the Holy Ghost as one of the things which Jesus would do; he presents the work of Jesus as comprehended in the two things I have spoken of—the Lamb of God that takes away sin, and He that baptizes with the Holy Ghost. So the Lord Himself, " If I go not away the Comforter will not come unto you, if I go away I will send him unto you." So again, " whom the Father will send in my name ;" when He is come he will reprove (convict) the world of sin, and righteousness, and judgment, guide the disciples into all truth, shew them things to come. So Peter, when He was come according to promise, " being by the right hand of God exalted, and having received of the Father the promise of the Holy Ghost [note this reception of it for others on His exaltation], he hath shed forth this which ye now see and hear ;" and when pricked in their hearts they asked, " Men and brethren, what shall we do?" he replies, " Repent, and be baptized, every one of you, for the remission of sins, and ye shall receive the gift of the Holy Ghost. For the promise is to you, and to your children, and to all that are afar off, even as many as the Lord our God shall call." So, before the priests, " We are witnesses of these things, and so also is the Holy Ghost which is given to them that obey him." So to Cornelius, God gives the proof that He will have the Gentiles by giving him the Holy Ghost, so that Peter could not forbid water. So at Samaria, they all receive the Holy Ghost by means of Peter and John, having been baptized by Philip. In the case referred to in Acts xix., Paul says, "Have ye received the Holy Ghost since ye believed?" Peter, describing the order of dispensations, speaks of the prophets finding that the things they prophesied were not for them, neither have we got them, they are reported unto you, he says, by them that have preached the gospel unto you with the Holy Ghost sent down from heaven; wherefore be sober and hope to the end for the grace that is to be brought to you at the revelation of Jesus Christ.

These are ample to shew that the presence of the Holy Ghost, founded on the work of Christ and His exaltation, was the distinctive character of Christianity; the blessings connected with it run through the New Testament; the love of God shed abroad in our hearts, the knowledge that we are in Christ and Christ in us, the knowing that we are sons, so that we cry, Abba, Father —nay, dwelling in God, and God in us. True holy liberty, true divine knowledge, all and every enjoyment of blessings, and abounding in hope, and help in our infirmities, are attributed to the Holy Ghost; our good fruits are the fruits of the Spirit; our joy is joy in the Holy Ghost; our love, love in the Spirit; it is by one Spirit through Christ we have access to the Father; "If any man have not the Spirit of Christ he is none of his;" and this is Christ being in us.

All this shews to an attentive mind that it is distinctive of the Christian, but though it be the bright and blessed side I must not dwell on this further, but cite what FORMALLY shews it to be distinctive of the Christian; it is, "If we are led of the Spirit, we are not under law;" our bodies are the temple of the Holy Ghost which we

B

have of God ; we are not to grieve the Holy Spirit of God, by which we are sealed for the day of redemption. What is the appeal of the apostle to the Galatians connected with justification by faith ? "This only would I learn of you, received ye the Spirit by the works of the law or by the hearing of faith? Are ye so foolish, having begun in the Spirit, are ye now made perfect in the flesh?" They were slipping away through Judaizing teachers, teachers of the law, who were subverting, we read, whole houses, from justification by faith, and his appeal, as that which they all knew, is to their having received the Holy Ghost, not that they all walked well, but that the Holy Ghost was come, and that they had received it.

It may be said, But they who ministered the Spirit to them, an expression much to be noted, worked miracles. But *all* knew they had the Holy Ghost: if the flesh lusted in them, it lusted against the Spirit. In Romans a Christian is described as he that is after the Spirit; they were not in the flesh, their old Adam standing, but in the Spirit, if the Spirit of God *dwelt in them.* If any man had not the Spirit of Christ, he was none of His ; and this is not mere temper, for he continues, "and if Christ be in you, the body is dead because of sin, and the Spirit is life because of righteousness"—the Christian state was the effect of Christ being in them. It is by one Spirit we are all baptized into one body ; we are also builded together for a habitation of God through the Spirit.

But it is not my object to draw all the consequences of the presence of the Holy Ghost, but merely to shew that Christianity was characterized by it, even if they walked badly ; they grieved the Holy Spirit of God by which they were sealed unto the day of redemption. It is not surprising. The Father sending the Son was the grand and mighty basis of Christianity, and the sending of the Spirit, by both the Father and a glorified Christ, was a witness of His Lordship and exaltation, and the great testimony in the world, and that by which we know the value of the work and exaltation of One, and our relationship with the other, as sons, by grace with Him; that by which all was received here. Such was Christianity essentially in its basis. There were other collateral truths, of course, and important ones too, but these formed its base, not only for our blessing, but for the full revelation of God, Father, Son, and Holy Ghost.

There were directions for order, and simple ordinances clearly referred to, as two, baptism and the Lord's supper; both telling of Christ's death, one initiatory, the other continual; man judged, for Christ had been rejected, and redemption accomplished in His death. I refer to them now simply to shew that I acknowledge them fully and their value.

As a rule, elders and deacons were appointed in the various assemblies; ministry consisted in the exercise of gift, the gifts of the Spirit, who distributed to every man severally as He would, and each gifted person was a member of Christ's body, and exercised it according to scriptural order under the authority of Christ. The directions are found in 1 Corinthians, where there is no appearance of the existence of any elders at all. But such was Christianity as presented to us in scripture in its essential features. Has it preserved them? Is what is now called the church that Christianity, the system I find there?

The Christianity we find in scripture is, saints justified,

no sin imputed to them, perfected for ever, knowing they were forgiven and were sons, having personal consciousness of their relationship with God, accepted in the beloved, having full assurance of faith and hope, a confidence they were warned to hold fast ; and, as to service, gifts from on high, through the power of the Holy Ghost, imposed on every one the duty of service according to the gift he had received and the order prescribed in the word. If he had two talents or five talents, he was to trade with them—a wicked and slothful servant if he did not ; as every man had received the gift, he was so to minister the same, as good stewards of the manifold grace of God ; women were to keep silence in the assemblies ; men were to exercise their gifts according to prescribed order; these gifts were set in the whole church at large, and exercised according to God's will, as a distinct member of the one whole body. Some were signs of power (as to which there is no promise of continuance), others, the fruit of Christ's faithful care of His body—two of these being the foundation—to continue till we all come to the measure of the stature of the fulness of Christ : besides this, the edifying and growth of the body was carried on by that which every joint supplied, according to the effectual working in the measure of every part.

Such was the christian state scripturally, known personal relationship with God, according to the efficacy of Christ's redemption, and the Holy Ghost given to each and working in each as seemed good to Him, Christ giving from on high assuredly what was needed for the accomplishment of the assembly as His body, and these gifts operating in those that had them as members of the one body, and set in the assembly as a whole, in no way local. Besides this, and baptism and the Lord's supper, by one of which they were received into God's house, and by the other both the unity of the body and Christ's death were symbolized, there were local officers, elders appointed in every city. They were local offices, not gifts, though gifts they might have, and one was desirable to make their service in their office more effectual ; but these were local, the gifts were not.

The church, as understood in modern times in all its compartments, is constituted, has its existence by, and is based upon, the clergy and its sacraments, not an accomplished redemption and the presence and power of the Holy Ghost; a clergy, which is called the ministry, and even the church. I take as a plain, popular proof of the truth of this, the Evangelical Alliance ; it abhors the corruption that has entered into the church, but it would not admit Quakers and Plymouth Brethren : the former reject clergy and sacraments, the latter clergy only, holding baptism and the Lord's supper, both insisting on ministry by the Spirit. I am not insisting now on their being right or wrong, I merely take it as a popular proof of the basis of the universal system, even where gross corruptions are resisted. It results in this, that the recognition of a clergy is the basis of the church, the *sine quâ non*, the essential condition.

I am not, remark here, speaking of the corruption of the church; this was so great, that Nicholas Clemangis, the greatest man of his age in the middle ages, declares that putting a girl into a convent was making her a prostitute ; unnatural crimes were usual with the clergy, and Baronius declares that for a hundred years he cannot recognize the popes as legitimate popes at all, save for dates. They were not elected by the clergy, nor approved even by their vote, but put in by the mistresses of the marquises of Tuscany, sometimes those who were sons of a previous pope by their mothers, after his death. And it came to fightings even at the moment of consecration, and, as whichever got the upper hand broke all the ordinations of the one whom he had driven out, a book was written to reassure people as to having any sacraments at all.

But this was the corruption of the church, and I do not enter into it. It is no wonder that the Holy Ghost, as scripture testifies of it, was utterly turned away from. My thesis is, not that the church as now held historically was corrupted, but that the church so held was itself the total departure in principle from scripture, from what Christ set up by the Holy Ghost. The doctrine of full justification by faith, founded on accomplished redemption, and the recognition of the Holy Ghost as present and a directing power, were lost, and the clergy and sacraments substituted for them. The reformation removed many corruptions which had grown intolerable, and many false principles, but the notion of the church was still based on the clergy and the sacraments. It is hard to prove a negative; but it is quite certain that neither a full redemption, nor, though the words be used once or twice, a complete possessed justification by faith, as Paul teaches it, a perfecting for ever by its one offering, a known personal acceptance in Christ, is ever found in any ecclesiastical writings after the canonical scriptures for long centuries. We have Barnabas saying they had forgiveness of sins by baptism (chap. xi.): this, note, was only previous sins, administrating a great blessing surely, but not the definite acceptance in Christ of a person to whom the Lord imputes no sin so that there was no condemnation.* There was no trace of any full justification by faith, though, of course, Christ is owned as having come and having died as the Saviour, along with a mass of strange allegorical interpretations.

He calls Christianity a new law; we have a very meagre reference to His dying for the forgiveness of our sins (chap. v.), but he insists on the cross and water going together (chap. xi.), that is, baptism, putting their trust in the cross, descend into the water; we go down into the water full of sins and pollutions, but come up again bringing forth fruit.

He refers to the serpent of brass, but it is looking to Christ as able to give life. He says, too, as regards God's dwelling in us, having received remission of our sins, and trusting in the name of the Lord, we are become renewed, being again created, as it were, from the beginning, wherefore God truly dwells in our house, that is, in us. But how does He dwell in us? the word of faith, the calling of His promise, the wisdom of His righteous judgments, &c., &c.

Now I have quoted all this because, while the epistle is so full of absurdities, that people have denied that it is of Barnabas, and one sees how one falls down a precipice after we leave inspiration, yet it has by far the most truth of any of these old writings. His attributing for-

---

* An expression which distinctly marks the difference between forgiveness by a sacrament and personal acceptance in Christ. The question arose, and was regularly debated, if sins could be forgiven afterwards; and in Hermas, already remission, and repentance afterwards, are distinguished; and in Tertullian, when Montanists contended against forgiving an adulterer, forgiveness by baptism was administrative and for the past; the acceptance of the person wholly a different thing, and never thought of.

giveness of sins to baptism is very natural; for when a heathen or a Jew became professedly a Christian by baptism, he did administratively enter into the privileges belonging to Christianity, though this became soon the doctrine of the efficiency of the sacrament. But I cannot doubt that the writer was a Christian, and though despised by many ancient and modern writers, and the departure from the true christian standing, from a gospel such as Paul's, who was not sent to baptize, is flagrantly evident, still, it contains by far the most truths of any of these ancient writers. I have quoted all that is of worth; the rest is really nonsense in general.

Besides this, he makes us hasten to our appointed place by our works, and then gives a string of commandments to follow, among which he tells them to labour with their hands to give to the poor, that their sins might be forgiven them, and these commandments were the way of light. We get here some very faint trace of the first elements of the gospel, but the application of the blessing of it is by baptism and works, but he is pretty much on the 'ground of the historic church. Be ye taught, he says, of God, seeking what it is the Lord requires of you, and doing it, that ye may be saved in the day of judgment: we have nothing of the clergy. The epistle is found attached to the New Testament in the MSS, as in Sinaiticus, along with Hermas; he distinctly substitutes (ii.) men's offering themselves for the burnt-offerings, and quotes the prophets as putting man's conduct in the place of sacrifices. It is an utter departure from the gospel as found in scripture, with happy signs that he did not intend to deny it.

In Polycarp we have one of the best of these epistles. and he quotes Paul to the Ephesians: "Knowing that by grace ye are saved, not by works, but by the faith of God, through Jesus Christ," again making it vague. We have no recognition of the Holy Ghost; I do not mean he denies it. It is forgotten; but the clergy (though he has not a notion of episcopacy in an individual, nor writes as such, but the contrary) are fully recognized, "being subject to the priests and deacons as unto God and Christ." In fine, there is no harm in the epistle, not a trace of the gospel save the quotation of Paul, Christ's death being used as an example, no recognition of the Holy Ghost or any gift of the Spirit, but a full recognition of the clergy.

As to Clement, we have a long exhortation to peace: the blood of Christ is owned, it is precious to God, and has obtained the grace of repentance for the whole world, is given for us. (xxi., xlix.) If we walk right, obey the commands of God, we shall get the blessing, as all the ancient worthies. (vii., ix.) Faith he refers to, but only acting by faith to get the blessing. "For what (xxxii.) was our father Abraham blessed? was it not because that through faith he wrought righteousness?" He says we are not justified by our own wisdom or by the works which we have done in the holiness of our hearts, but by that faith by which God Almighty justified all men from the beginning. (xxxii.) As to the clergy, he owns no bishop at Corinth—this is very marked in the letter; like Polycarp, he owns presbyters only; his letter would have been a flagrant disrespect if there had been one, and he states that the apostles appointed presbyters, but he knew no prelacy. But he is the first to introduce what soon corrupted the church: in insisting on order he refers to the chief-priest, priests, Levites, and laymen; this he speaks of as Jewish, and only by

B 2

way of illustration; still, it gave the direction to thought.
So he speaks of offerings at the appointed seasons and
the appointed place: God has ordained by His supreme
will and authority both where and by what persons they
are to be performed. (xl.) In a word, the full doctrine
of redemption and peace is dropped, the Holy Ghost, as
a present thing, unknown (he refers to the Corinthians
having had a great effusion of the Holy Ghost), and the
clergy set up distinctly, and that on the pattern of Judaism. Two things are objected to in him, and that even
as long ago as Photius, that he was unsound as to the
divinity of Christ, and the Phœnix. We easily see that
the power of the Holy Ghost as inspiration was gone,
so that the mere reference to the Phœnix is nothing ex-
traordinary; what is to me in the matter is, that he
refers to heathen priests and their inquiries as true knowledge and, so to speak, divine matters, and the miracle
of the Phœnix appears as a plain sanction of heathenism.

As to the divinity of Christ, he is, to say the least,
cloudy. It has been answered he calls Him the sceptre
of the divine Majesty. This does not prove much,
rather worse than nothing. Christ is throughout a man,
a priest prescribing our offerings, and, what is strange,
quoting Hebrews i., he says, "But unto the Son, saith the
Lord, thou art my Son, this day have I begotten thee,
ask of me," &c. It cannot, perhaps, be said that he
denied the Deity of the Lord, but it certainly is not in
his mind, he is insensible to it, he thinks of the blessed
Lord in another way; a full known salvation by grace
he most assuredly knows not; there is no present Holy
Ghost in his mind; and he sets up the clergy on the
pattern of Judaism. His epistle is a distinct revelation

of where Christians had got to. It is relied on for justi-
fying the present state of the church; prelacy it does
not justify, it has no trace of such a thing, or of any individual episcopacy, but it does picture the general state,
in its germinal principles: but it does not speak of a full
redemption and peace; not a word of what Paul teaches
of our standing as Christians, nothing : nor of the presence of the Holy Ghost; the clergy, and offerings at
an appointed place, he insists on, quoting Judaism and
the order of an army as a pattern and authority.

Further, Paul's doctrine as to the Holy Ghost and
ministry are so completely ignored as to place these points
on ground which obliterates and denies all Paul's teaching (xiii.) : he says, " The apostles brought us the good
news of the gospel from the Lord Jesus Christ, Jesus Christ
from God." Now this ignores the Holy Ghost and the whole
of that form of Christianity which resulted from Christ's
exaltation. The blessed Lord says, " I have many things
to say to you, but ye cannot bear them now, but when
he the Spirit of truth is come he will guide you into all
truth." This Clement wholly ignores. But Paul flatly
contradicts Clement's statement : I neither received it—
speaking of the gospel he preached—of man, neither
was I taught it, but by the revelation of Jesus Christ:
and this in Galatians i. 2, when he is carefully setting
aside any connection with a derivation of office or truth
from the apostles. He was sent forth from Antioch, it
is expressly said, by the Holy Ghost, and this is so true,
that he does not recognize the apostles as sent forth by
Christ on earth, but only as gifts from Christ when
ascended. (Eph. iv. 10, 11.) " He that descended is
the same also that ascended up far above all heavens,
that he might fill all things, and he gave some, apostles,"

&c. The apostles, during the lifetime of Christ, were forbidden to go to the Gentiles (Matt. x.), and the mission they received (Matt. xxviii.) after Christ's resurrection, not after His ascension, they relinquished to Paul. (Gal. ii. 8, 9.) However, I do not dwell on this, but the assertion of Clement denies the whole ministry and power of the Holy Ghost, as sent down from on high, after Christ's exaltation, and the truths into which He led the apostles, even the twelve themselves, and which Christ declares they could not bear when He was with them, and into which the Holy Ghost would lead them. So, as to power, too, Luke xxiv. 49.

As to Ignatius, little need be said. In the Syriac epistles there is no allusion to any gospel truth at all; in the shorter Greek ones, generally received till the Syriac were found, we find an allusion to salvation by the fruits of the cross, in that to the Smyrnæans. (i., ii.) But still, as in that to the Ephesians, it is sacramental forgiveness. Christ was born and baptized, that through His passion He might sanctify water, to the washing away of sin. He suffered for us that we might be saved. He is sound in the faith, denounces the gnostics and teachers of the Jewish law, but the doctrine of redemption and peace there is not a trace of, nor of the presence of the Holy Ghost in the believer. As to the clergy, the Greek epistles are a tissue of bombastical laudations, declaring that, apart from the bishop, they were without God and away from every blessing. In the Syriac, in the epistle to Polycarp, we have, "Look to the bishop, that God also may look upon you. I will be instead of the souls of those who are subject to the bishop, and the presbyters, and the deacons: with them may I have a portion with God."

As to sacraments, I am not aware that he speaks of baptism; a passage in the Epistle to the Romans may refer to the Lord's supper, or not. In Syriac, "I do not desire the food of corruption, neither the desires of this world; the bread of God I seek, which is the flesh of Jesus Christ, and His blood I seek, which is love incorruptible;" in Greek, "I delight not in the food of corruption, nor in the pleasures of this life; I desire the bread of God, the heavenly bread, the bread of life, which is the flesh of Jesus Christ, the Son of God, who was born in these last days of the seed of David and Abraham; and the drink of God which I desire is His blood, which is incorruptible love and eternal life." He had said, my love is crucified. It is hard to say exactly what he means, his language is so outrageously mystical and exaggerated. Thus he talks of being fervent in the blood of God. One thing is clear, that in about fifty years after the destruction of Jerusalem, and Clement and Barnabas, episcopacy had got strong hold of some minds. Ignatius seemed to have been inflamed by some divisions or difficulties, if the Greek epistles are genuine; but, while quite orthodox, the small dying remains of the sense of salvation to be found fifty years before were pretty much lost altogether, and the doctrine of the clergy ripened, as constituting the church.

Hermas remains. Here all thought of divine truth is gone, and baptism and nonsensical heresy reign triumphant, with the proof that the system of immoral asceticism was grown up in the professing church, to say nothing of lying visions. He sees a tower, which is the church; but this tower is made up of the apostles, bishops, and doctors and ministers. Then there were those who had suffered for the Lord's name, and are fallen asleep; then young ones are built in, but some who had sinned were cast out, and would be put into the tower if they repented. But there were those which fell by the water, and could not get in—they had doubted; these may repent, and be in a lower rank, but not in this tower. The water is clearly baptism; the builders are angels. Faith is one of seven virtues, only the first; and those that hold fast to their works shall have a place in the tower. In fourth command (iii.) we are forgiven by baptism; then he hath one repentance granted him, if he sins more he shall hardly live; man has two angels, one suggests evil, the other good. If a man is sad in an evil sort, this vexes the Holy Spirit who dwells in him, and the Spirit entreats God, and leaves him. All this part is wholly of works and man's will, listening to the good Spirit in him.

In the fifth similitude he represents the work of Christ thus:—A man had a farm, set his servant to stake the vineyard. This he did, but of his own good will dug it, and pulled up the weeds; the master finding this, then takes counsel with his son and the angels what he should do, as the servant had done more than was required; so he makes the servant heir with the son. The master is the Creator, and the son is the Holy Ghost; the stakes, those set over His people to support them; the friends called to counsel are the angels; the servant is Christ, who was set to have their messengers to support the people, but of His own mind suffered to blot out their offences. God placed in a chosen body, in which God should dwell, the Holy Spirit, which was created first of all. This body, therefore, into which the Holy Spirit was brought served that Spirit, walking rightly and purely in modesty, nor ever defiled that Spirit; and as

He had served this Holy Spirit without blame, and done more than he was set to do, he was made heir with the master's son.

He seems to have had some scruple about his statements, for he answers the objection as to putting the Son of God there, that He was put in a place of authority to set His messengers over those the Father had delivered to Him. His instructor adds, he must keep his body clean and pure. Hermas then asks, what if, through ignorance, he had already defiled his Holy Spirit? His instructor replies, as for men's former actions which through ignorance they have committed, God only can afford a remedy unto them, for all power belongeth unto Him; but now guard thyself; and seeing God is Almighty and merciful, He will grant a remedy to what thou hast formerly done amiss, if for the time to come thou shalt not defile thy body and spirit.

In the ninth similitude (xvi.), we find, if, indeed, I understand it, the dead of the Old Testament, though already dead, were sealed with baptism, or they could not be built into the tower, the church; how is somewhat obscure, but it seems the apostles and teachers, when they died, went down to the dead, and put the seal of baptism on them, so they came up alive with them. (viii. 3.)

The great tree .... is the law of God published throughout the whole earth. Now this law is the Son of God, who is preached to all the ends of the earth. .... The great and venerable angel was Michael, who has power over this people, and governs them; for he has planted the law in the hearts of those who have believed; and therefore visits those to whom he has given the law, to see if they have kept it.

The immoral asceticism to which I have alluded. I have, on the whole, decided to leave out. It is a fact well known by readers of ecclesiastical history, under the title of παρεισακταί, or subintroductæ. The only importance of introducing it here was the public sanction given to a most vile and abominable practice; for Hermas was read in the Churches. This Hermas was brother to Pope Pius I. (of old he was thought to be he whom Paul speaks of), and he lived about forty to sixty years after the death of the apostle John.

Now, I have really given the very best things that are said in Barnabas, Clement, and Polycarp, and the other two, if good, can be spoken of in Ignatius and Hermas. Some of old rejected Barnabas; the others have hardly been called in question as to genuineness. Some call Hermas inspired, as Origen: Irenæus quotes it as scripture. Now, genuine or not, Hermas and Clement were read in the churches; not in result put in the canon, still were added at the end of the manuscripts of the New Testament, as Barnabas and Hermas in the Sinaitic, Clement in the Alexandrian, and so on. I do not know that Ignatius' epistles ever were; he was a martyr, and eager for martyrdom. Nor do I know that Polycarp's was; but in the early church it was a question as to most of them whether they were scripture or not; they were of the next highest authority, and some unquestionably constantly read in the churches. If Ignatius' Latin or Greek ones are spurious, the Syriac are there, and quite enough: nobody doubts that he wrote epistles —seven, it is said; nobody doubts that the primitive church teemed with forgeries and falsifications to prop up the system I refer to, and other foolish or evil things.

But we have enough to shew that immediately after the apostles, beginning with Clement, Paul's companion, whose epistles no one questions, Barnabas, of the same date, whoever wrote it, soon after 70; Ignatius, some say 106, others 116; Polycarp at the same date; Hermas some 50 years later; we have a collection of writings which express the then current thoughts and views, and which were more or less publicly read. Now, in these writings we do not find a trace of the gospel, and redemption and salvation, and blessings, which are found in Galatians, Romans, Colossians, Ephesians, 2 Corinthians, John, or even Peter, who does not go so far as Paul and John; nor do we find the practical recognition of the Holy Ghost; I speak of their teachings. Polycarp and Ignatius were, no doubt, saints; Barnabas and Clement, it may be, too, though in the last less appears; yet I would not call it in question. On the other hand, the clergy and sacraments, particularly baptism (Paul was not sent to baptize), are the constituent elements of the church they are conversant with. They own Christ's death, of course, but its effect or application, and the Christian's place, as Paul and other apostles put it, is nowhere found.

It is not the fact that there are elders, of course, that makes the sudden departure from scriptural truth and standing evident. Paul chose such, but that they and sacraments are everything—constitute the church; and what constituted Christianity as God gave it is gone.

All this led the way to hierarchical power, and finally to Popery in the West; and, as to practice, the deliberate adoption of heathenism, days and months and years, formally judged in Galatians as a return to heathenism, and the deliberate substitution of saints' memories, as they were called, for those of demi-gods—places of memorial, where they feasted and got drunk in honour of saints instead of demi-gods, that at least, as Augustine expresses it, their drunkenness might be consecrated to saints, not to demons; and this was deliberately done everywhere, formally allowed in England, where temples were changed into churches; and these festivals were the origin of our village wakes: Christmas was the dissolute feast of the Lupercalia.

But all these things were the fruits of this departure from Christianity. I speak of the departure itself; it had not come to this in Clement's and Barnabas' time, but the church, such as it is historically known and thought of to-day, had been substituted for Christianity.

I may sum up the system in the words of a writer long subsequent, as briefly stating the system, using another's translation: "Whereas the human race, by the demerit derived to it from the fault of the first sinner, had become pierced with the darts of eternal punishment. . . . . Christ granted to it certain remedial sacraments, to the end that it might acknowledge the difference between what is merited by nature and what it received by grace, and that as nature could bring punishment only, grace, not called grace if granted to merit, might furnish whatever appertains to salvation." This is its ripe formulary. The system began as soon as the apostles were gone.

There were two departures from truth: heresy, particularly, at first, gnosticism—this ends in antichrist; and a human view of the church, with the practical denial of the Christian's place by the Spirit; the last ends in Babylon. This takes essentially the character of the clergy, and the Spirit being with them; and so of the sacramental system as the channels of special grace. We may now see what light the New Testament throws on this subject; but history and the writings of the apostolic fathers, so called, from Clement to Hermas, shew us plainly that the doctrine of the Christian's place in Christ, and of the Holy Ghost present and active in all saints, as also freely distributing His gifts as He will, was totally lost at once by Christians after the apostles were gone. I am not denying that there was a set of people gathered, which gathering, in fact, continued, and was corrupted gradually; that is clear, but that from the outset this gathered body of men lost the place, position, and power of that in which they had been established, and that the principles on which the gathering stood and was held to exist were, as soon as placed on their own responsibility, the contrary of what God had set them on. That it was not a body of persons knowing themselves to be in Christ, exalted as man at the right hand of God, consequent upon His having redeemed them, and perfected them for ever, for whom there was no condemnation, every one of whom was anointed and sealed by the Holy Ghost come down from heaven, the earnest of the inheritance which they had not yet, which Holy Ghost, uniting them into one body, and distributing to every man severally as He would, made each servants of Christ in his place and gift, and responsible to trade with the talent confided to him; and as every man had received the gift so to minister the same; but a body of persons who were viewed as connected with a clergy, who might or might not be gifted, but their connection with whom formed them into one corporation, of which the administration of the sacraments formed the bond and link, and who by their works were to obtain salvation at the end.

Now this was really the Judaism against which the apostle so earnestly contended, and which met and harassed him in his service in every place, which would have a derived, ordained ministry, disowning the power and title of the Spirit, and the true Lordship of Christ, and teaching justification by works, apostolic succession, and the observing of days, and months, and years.

Was this departure from Christ to be expected at once, or was the successional continuance of the outward body that which was secured by the Lord's promise? What does the word declare? Heresy fully contributed its part; but, whatever was the cause, was the continuance of the body under God's approbation contemplated or not? Let us see what was the state of things even before the apostle's death. " All they which be in Asia have turned away from me; all seek their own, not the things of Jesus Christ; the mystery of iniquity doth already work." So Paul. Peter says, "The time is come that judgment shall begin at the house of God." Jude, " False brethren have crept in unawares." Was this to be remedied? " These are they," he says, " of whom Enoch, the seventh from Adam, prophesied, saying, The Lord cometh, with ten thousand of his saints, to execute judgment." So John, " Ye have heard that antichrist cometh, and already there are many antichrists, whereby we know that it is the last time." All this before the apostles were gone—Peter, expecting no proper successional care, writing that " they might have these things always in remembrance;" Jude having " to contend earnestly for the faith once delivered to the saints;" James telling them " to be patient to the coming of the

Lord, that the judge was at the door;" Peter, that delay was not " slackness concerning promise, but the long-suffering of God, not willing that any should perish;" the Lord Himself, hanging all in suspense over them, saying words, already then misinterpreted, " If I will that he tarry till I come;" but all marking the decay and ruin, and teaching to look forward to the coming of the Lord.

But Paul, especially the apostle of the church, and who alone, indeed, formally speaks of it, gives us more precise and definite statements. " I know that after my decease grievous wolves shall enter in, not sparing the flock, yea, even of your own selves shall perverse men arise to draw away the disciples after them; wherefore watch, and remember," &c. &c.; thought of a successor, in these days called bishop, he had none; the existence of such, then or after his departure, is a thing unknown to him. He commends them to God and the word of His grace (compare the language of Ignatius in similar circumstances), which was able to build them up, and give them an inheritance among all them that are sanctified. The time, he tells us, would come when they would not endure sound doctrine, but after their own lusts heap to themselves teachers having itching ears, and they shall turn away their ears from the truth, and be turned unto fables. This, mark, is a general character of the state of things. There were many unruly and vain talkers and deceivers, specially they of the circumcision, whose mouths must be stopped, who subvert whole houses. The result he fully states in 2 Timothy iii., " that in the last days perilous times should come," and then, giving a description answering to that in which he shews the state of heathenism, he closes by saying, " having the form of godliness, but denying the power of it?" but at the close of the chapter, he says, " Evil men and seducers shall wax worse and worse, deceiving and being deceived," and then refers to Timothy's having learnt the truth from himself, and the power and authority of the scriptures as a safeguard.

The tares which the devil sowed in the field were to remain till harvest ; the mystery of iniquity already working in the apostle's days would go on and ripen into the man of sin, and end in judgment ; when the message comes from Christ, through John, to the churches, they have no authority, but are judged, and the Christian is called upon to hear what the Spirit says to them ; they were not competent to speak or guide, but he that had ears to hear was to listen to the judgment pronounced on them, to what was said. No voice of any universal church was to guide, but the individual to listen to the voice of testimony, as to what was found in the church. The church did not judge, or guide, or teach, but the word revealed Christ's judgment of this church, and to that he who had ears was to listen.

The Gentiles have not continued in God's goodness, and are to be cut off. But the origin of all this was, they having begun in the Spirit, ended in the flesh. The clergy replaced the power and gifts of the Spirit, the sacraments His grace, and the clergy being the ministry ; the free distribution of the Holy Ghost, and the exercise of gift, where gift was, was set aside. The apostolic order was set aside, as the christian position before God was lost, both connected with the presence of the Holy Ghost, as the expectation of God's Son from heaven was soon dropped out ; men ceased to watch for Him.

All the principles which constituted Christianity under

apostolic teaching were lost in the body left behind them; the place of Christians in Christ, known by the Holy Ghost, His free presence and power working in living streams in individual Christians, under the authority of Christ, regulated by the word, and constant expectation of Christ from heaven. These were the principles of the church on earth, as established by God; what is called the church is the denial of all these, only the last was lost later than the others. But the church *system* was founded on an ordained clergy, with whom rested all ministry, and the sacraments as that which incorporated the laity under them, and thereby the *establishment* of the church on *earth*, not waiting for God's Son from *heaven*.

I am not denying the existence of elders, or of baptism and the Lord's supper; what I insist on is, that what has taken place is the substitution of these for the principles on which God founded His assembly in the world, and that this was immediate. The historical church is man's system, from the beginning, in contrast with God's; that system has been corrupted, but what has been corrupted is man's system, not God's. No doubt God had gathered the first materials into unity, but the principles on the which He founded His assembly resisted, specially by Judaism, during the life of the apostles, were given up when they were gone; and the system *they* had resisted became that which stood before men's eyes as the church. The free power of the Spirit, and known acceptance in an exalted Christ, ceased to be the constituent principles of those gathered; the clerical principle denying the Spirit, making elders the ministry as a clergy, that is, ordained teachers, not the gift and power of the Holy Ghost. This was first developed in local episcopacy, then in diocesan episcopacy and the hierarchy, and then in Popery.

We are called on by God to go to the scriptures, which are abiding truth, knowing the Holy Ghost was to abide with us for ever. Our choice is between, on one side, the authority of the word and the Holy Ghost, connected with what is called the universal priesthood of Christians, an incorrect application of an important truth ; on the other, the infallible pope, or infidelity, the crown of the system of the clergy; or the no longer disguised enmity of the human heart against God and His word. Only remark, the word of God and the Spirit of God, as acting in all saints, is alike set aside by both. The abominations in which the departure I signalize, abominations worthy of, yea, worse than heathenism, in the professing church resulted, are known to those acquainted with ecclesiastical history, but that is not my object now ; but it is well that he who is not familiar with that history should know, that the very vilest and most degraded evil of which history has preserved the record is found in the history of what is called the church of God.

G. Morrish, Printer, 24, Warwick Lane, Paternoster Row, E. C.

www.ingramcontent.com/pod-product-compliance
Lightning Source LLC
Chambersburg PA
CBHW081305040426
42452CB00014B/2657